Introduction of Dear Congress by Simone Ilese:

In this unique era of political turmoil facing the United States, I decided the best way to exercise my First Amendment right was by using my pen and e-mailing concerns to congressional representatives. With continuing threats of constitutional issues being stripped away and damage being done to our great nation, like so many other Americans, it was my way of standing up and voicing my views. Watching the current occupant in the presidential office trample over the media, not tell the truth, and work towards reducing our constitutional rights and civil liberties was and continues to be shocking. While some members of Congress remain silent and continually enable the ongoing damage to our country, the power still remains in all of us, as private citizens, to make our contributions. It does not matter how, as long as we are contributing by publicly protesting, running for office, actively participating in political parties or helping with the upcoming midterm elections. As I no longer wanted to feel like we are heading for a dictatorship that only allows bowing and praising an undisciplined and inadequate leader, I wanted to exercise my First Amendment right. So, I wrote this short book, hoping other Americans will be inspired to use their pens or voices to exercise their First Amendment rights to their congressional representatives.

Prologue of Dear Congress by Simone Ilese:

All my life, I was moved by social injustices, constitutional law, and civil rights. At an early age, I thought I had a passion for law and wanted to become an attorney. I loved writing early in my education. In high school, I enjoyed debate and initiated an anti-nuclear energy campaign.   With my passion for writing and social injustices, I majored in English and minored in political science. So, I went to law school, and spent most of my career as a prosecutor.   Also, I terminated parental rights for the Department of Health and Rehabilitative Services and handled other areas of law. Later on, I spent ten years teaching mostly online law classes to college students all over the country.

Ironically, I was born on Constitution Day, a celebration of our Constitution, September 17th. I wrote this book because I was tired of hearing the POTUS constantly attack the media for not praising him and trying to suppress our First Amendment rights. I wanted to exercise my First Amendment rights.

Inspired by the tumultuous times in the current presidential administration, I vented my anger at the outrageous acts of corruption, immortality, and inhumanity, and incompetence through my writing. I wrote letters via emails to my congressional representatives from the Senate and House. With so many pressing issues, it felt so overwhelming to have a government seeming more like a dictatorship with no one really fighting against it. I did not run for political office. Instead, I joined my local democratic affiliated organizations and became an active voice.

Also, I continually sent letters through emails to anyone who would listen. I wondered even if the lengthy responses I received were standard responses to everyone.   Even sending a letter to the editor seemed futile, as I wondered if anyone reads newspapers anymore. As I write this book, I only did this to share my ideas because I did not know if anyone was listening to the cries against an unjust administration like we have never seen before in U.S. history.

As my English teacher mother always said, "the pen is mightier than the sword." Everyone in the media are loudly voicing their concerns, but is anyone listening? So that is what I am doing, using my pen in the most well-intentioned, thought provoking way.

Dear Congresswoman,

Congratulations on winning the election as our new Congresswoman!!! My husband and I voted for you and attended your recent lecture at the College. We immensely enjoyed hearing your moving story about you and your family as immigrants and your courageous aspirations to enter the life of politics.

As a Democrat all of my life and raised in a family with Democratic ideals, I strongly share your sentiments. My grandparents were Russian immigrants, one of them, my maternal grandmother, barely speaking English when she first entered the U.S. and married my grandfather. My paternal grandfather escaped the Bolshevik Revolution when he was a young teen helping his family follow him and escape persecution from his country to the U.S. My husband's father was a Polish immigrant who spent 3 years in a concentration camp before he escaped as a teen after his entire family were killed by the Nazis.

My husband's mother and older sister were luckily sent to England before they were orphans and lost their parents and family to the Nazis.   Eventually, my husband's parents came to the U.S. where they met.

As a native Floridian, I grew up with an English teacher mom who always taught me, "it's not what you have, but it's what you do with what you have." So, I worked hard, graduated from law school at an early age, practiced as a lawyer for many years, including working as a county prosecutor. I took time off to raise young kids and tragically lost my father to lung cancer at a young age. So, I am not happy with the tobacco companies and did some civil litigation in that area. Both of my children are in college. My son was Valedictorian of a large local high school recently and is now studying electrical engineering and physics at 18 in junior level classes. My daughter graduated 2 years before and is 21, in graduate school, soon to become a tax accountant/CPA. For the past 9 years, I have been an adjunct professor teaching law classes, mostly online, to students all over the country at several colleges. I teach everything from criminal law, constitutional law, international to civil law classes. I love teaching the law, as often it relates to the current politics of our time. Just yesterday, in a class, we were discussing the executive orders, checks and balances, as it relates to the Constitution and congressional acts.

So, like millions of other citizens, I relate to your personal story and the issues on many levels. I strongly supported President Obama, and was shocked, distraught, and deeply upset when Hillary Clinton lost the election.   I knew that we had no choice, but to accept the current outcome, as difficult as it was. To see not only the dangerous rhetoric, but the actions to go from bad to worst continually shocks the conscience. Like you said in your Rollins lecture, that now is the time for a call to action, I believe in action, but feel a sense of helplessness in the state of the current politics. The issues seem overwhelming, not only in the number that need to be tackled, but in depth. From human rights, to individual rights, economics, environmental issues, I can only imagine as a new Congresswoman, the issues must seem unsurmountable at times. I am only a private citizen, not a politician, passionate about so many issues from gun control, women's rights, environmental protection; Democratic values.

At the recent lecture, I wanted to meet you, but did not get the opportunity. I live in your district with many nice people, but probably outnumbered by supporters for the current situation. My talents lie in communication, writing, speaking, and relating to others. Please let me know if there is anything I can do to make a difference. I wish you all of the luck in the world as our district's Congresswomen!

Simone Ilese

2/2/2017

Dear Congresswoman,

This is my second email letter, as my first one is posted below. Thanks for your continuing hard work. As mentioned, there are so many controversial issues with this new administration of great concern. One major issue is the lingering evidence of Russian ties between the administration and commander in chief that raise glaring red flags of conflict of interests and potentially a more dangerous relationship. So, my question is what efforts are being made by Congress, specifically the House of Representatives, to investigate these potentially dangerous relationships that could compromise the safety, welfare, and democratic ideals of our nations. Also, this relates to the interference with the Democratic party in the recent election and any efforts to obtain the POTUS's tax records as evidence.

Thanks in advance.

Simone Ilese

3/1/2017

Dear Congress,

I am one of your avid supporters. Watching the President's speech last night was like watching the wizard in the Wizard of Oz fake his powers. While he may have improved his tone, the message and substance were the same. It was not his words, but he was doing an acting job, like a phony salesman, delivering the white nationalist words of his assistants.

There was no detail for important issues like protecting national security, health care, the environment, and so many important issues. The problem with crime in this country is not the influx of immigrants, but access to guns. While there is no effort to legislate gun control, he does the opposite of what is best for this country in controlling gun violence, like sign a bill the same morning of the speech to give the mentally ill easier access to guns. His words to control gun violence in places like Chicago do not match his actions.

As a child, I grew up in Miami with an investigator father and English teacher mother. My father owned guns for his job. When I was six years old, my two year old brother got control of a loaded gun and pointed it at me. My mother got it away in time. Where are the statistics on gun deaths in America compared to other countries with better gun control?

I have a strong passion for these issues and many more. I worked in criminal law for many years as a former prosecutor, a current attorney, and currently an online law professor. For almost ten years, I have been instructing students all over the country in areas of constitutional law, criminal law, civil law, and so many related areas. I have no idea how to be an active Democrat, but continue to write letters and express my views to members of Congress.

I have also posted below my previous letters to members of the Senate and House for your viewing.

Simone Ilese

3/1/2017

Dear Congress,

I have so many questions for our legislators, given the political turmoil our country is going through. The most pressing one relates to gun control.

After so many mass shootings in America, including our schools, why is there not action being taken in the area of gun control? The evidence shows that a reduction in guns reduces violence and gun deaths, not only in states with increased gun control, but also in other countries. When it comes to protecting our Constitution, we should know that the laws of our land require judges to balance our rights. Just as our first amendment rights are not unlimited, the second amendment right is not unlimited. What is so sacred about unlimited gun rights over protection of human lives, not limited to our college, high school, middle school, elementary school kids? What about protection of all human lives of all ages in shopping centers, movies, theatre, sports events, music concerts, etc.?

Congress is constrained by law makers who do nothing but talk about improving background checks, but doing nothing, or preventing the mentally ill from getting guns, when the opposite is done through an executive action early in the presidency to increase the right of the mentally ill to get guns. Instead of reducing the influx of access to guns in our country, Congress is now voting to reduce the gun control laws by allowing carrying concealed weapons across state lines promoting a vigilante type justice. Lawmakers funded by the NRA are compromised and not interested in saving lives.

Why is anyone not listening to the students who survived the Parkland High School mass shooting? They may be our only hope. Why should an 18 year old be able to purchase a gun when there is no right to get alcohol at 18? Is a gun a lesser evil than alcohol? Why should an 18 year old or anyone be able to get an AR-15 or guns used like assault weapons in recent mass shootings? If we do not change our way of thinking and status quo persists, what makes anyone think that the epidemic of mass shootings will stop? We need gun control laws like bans on assault weapons like AR-15, the age for gun purchases should start at age 21, etc. In addition, voters need to know who to vote for in the upcoming midterm elections so that lawmakers compromised and funded by the NRA do not continue to carry out the agendas that result in loss of so many precious human lives.

To the law makers who try to blame the FBI for not following up on the tip that the student wrote on social media that he wants to be professional shooter, yes, that should be investigated and never happen again. But, that does not shift the burden of responsibility. The burden of responsibility falls on the law makers and Congress to enact real gun control laws because the rights of the gun owners should never outweigh the right to life, liberty, and pursuit of happiness. If our citizens, all ages, and students are in fear for our lives and safety in the most sacred environments – our schools, temples, churches, shopping malls, movie theatre, concerts, and in public arenas, how is our Constitutional ideal and principles being upheld?

Simone Ilese

2/18/2018

(also published in Heritage Florida Jewish News, as Letter to Editor, "Action Must be Taken on Gun Control NOW" on March 2, 2018)

Dear Congress,

The U.S. policy of children of all ages being separated from parents is outrageous, immoral, and unnecessary. The majority of these children are innocent bystanders seeking asylum trying to escape atrocities in other countries and survive. They are not terrorists or drug cartel pawns, as the lying administration would have their base believe. Instead of welcoming these immigrants like our lady of liberty did for our ancestors, our government is treating them like common criminals. Housing children in warehouses, separating them by medal cages, limiting their freedoms to enjoy fresh air, but most devastating is separating them from parents for an unknown length of time is a governmental abomination that should outrage every American citizen.

The government policy that effectually separates children from parents imposes the presumption of guilt, having to prove innocence, which is contrary to our Constitutional ideas. This reminds me of other acts of moral outrage in our history like the racial segregation, the Holocaust, and Japanese Americans in internment camps.

Surviving the Holocaust, my mother-in-law was 6 years old when her parents transported her and her older sister to England because of the beginning of degradation of and killing of Jews in Nazi Germany. Growing up most of her youth in an orphanage in England, my mother-in-law survived, but was scarred for life. She remembers the last letter she received from her father before her parents were killed in a concentration camp. As a child growing up in an orphanage, she would beg for candy in lieu of affection. Although my mother-in-law eventually came to the U.S. and had some normalcy with a married life and five children, it was not without struggle. She developed depression, diabetes, and other mental health struggles. The pediatric and psychological experts are stressing that separation of the immigrant children from their parents coming from a brutal situation in South American countries will cause short and long term stressor problems with these children. That is what happened to my mother-in-law.

Every member of Congress and American citizen should not forget the wailing cries of these children institutionalized by outrageous and horrible policies. Is history repeating itself like the Holocaust and the Japanese internment camps? The current administration has made no secret of its attitude of discrimination of people based on ancestry and recent reference to immigrants seeking asylum as an infestation in our country.

As an attorney for the Department of Health and Rehabilitative Services years ago, I terminated parental rights in cases of children being abused, abandoned, and neglected by parents. The abuse cases involved horrific facts. In this tumultuous administration, it now appears that the abuse is being committed by our government. I am ashamed to call it our government because it is no longer the government I once knew under our U.S. Constitution and Declaration of Independence.

The current administration initially chose to lie and say it has no control over the immoral policy to separate these children from parents under guise of treating immigrants as criminals. What is Congress going to do to act, reverse, and not forget the current atrocities? For the parents deported back, will the children and babies be lost forever or ever reunited? If parents are escaping atrocities in other countries for American asylum, they do not have the luxury of time to think of U.S. deterrence tactics to separate the children. Does the U.S. really want to be remembered as the lesser of two evils? To lie and blame immigrant parents for taking children on a dangerous trip when the greater danger they are facing is the threat of being killed in their own country, is the saddest travesty in this continuing saga of not accepting diversity in a great nation.

Simone Ilese

6/20/2018

Dear Congress,

The current administration continues to not only flaunt its abuse of power by total disregard for the U.S. Constitution, but show its unwavering incompetence. By undoing previous Obama policies out of spite and not substance, it is continually and actively taking steps to create a humanitarian crisis. From the mistreatment of Muslims through a Muslim ban, mistreatment of DACA recipients, total lack of concern over the health care of all American citizens and the environment, mistreatment of all immigrants as criminals and separation of migrant children from parents, how much longer can the current administration continue its violations against humanity?

Was the recent executive order to end separation of children from migrants at borders a sham order to appease the media and outraged Americans? The Zero Tolerance policy continuing to treat all immigrants seeking asylum as criminals is outrageous, immoral, and tyrannical. The news reports that 2,300 children are still separated from their migrant parents with no government plans to reunite the separated kids with their parents. It is outrageous to think that the migrant children separated from either deported parents or detained parents may never be reunited again.

If the government is restricting photographs being released to public and media of detention centers' treatment of parents and children, and preventing access to centers all over country to members of Congress, how is this not tantamount to suppression of the First Amendment? What about reports of mistreatment of children in some detention centers? The administration continually lies to Americans, like recently stating it did not have a separation policy when it really did, and reversed it the next day out of fear of reprisals from public pressure.

Where is the public outrage out of talk of placing migrant babies or toddlers into foster care and adoption without consent from parents? It is unthinkable that our country could permanently terminate the rights of immigrant parents seeking asylum without due process under our Constitution? If the government continues to violate its own constitutional ideals, can you imagine what our democratic allies must be thinking? How much longer can the current administration continue to act like a dictatorship without guidance of any humane principles allowing the President and administration to act out of impulse control, ignorance, incompetence, and lack of empathy for human rights other than their own?

Simone Ilese

Attorney (formerly worked for Dept. of HRS terminating parental rights of abused children)

6/21/2018

Dear Congress,

Not all detention centers for migrant children are equal. The best ones viewed by the administration allowed 2 hours a day of outdoor time. The worse ones are being withheld from the public and limited to media and democrats. Why are only government approved photos being released to Americans? What abuses is the government hiding?

We are hearing about tender age facilities and unknown facilities all over the country housing displaced children separated from parents. We hear news reports of 10 year old boys sobbing in cages separate from mothers in cages. Are these poor migrant parents and children, toddlers, and babies being treated like terrorists?

The callousness and total disregard for the human lives of children and future immigrant families is horrifying, un-American, and shocks the conscience! If a President cannot act properly and handle the job, isn't it time for Congress to take action. To just sit back and let it happen is unacceptable. It is pathetic to hear the news media broadcasters to appeal to the POTUS's family to do the right thing. It is unfair to rely on private institutions to rescue these children.

Contrary to the misconception created by the current administration, the majority of migrant families coming through Mexico are not criminals, animals, drug dealers, rapists, terrorists, or bad people. The majority of the migrant families are seeking asylum and escaping grave dangers in other countries. To label and treat every one of them as criminals is a grave violation of our Constitution and American values.

 Even if the children are returned to parents, the reality of short and long term effects on the brain affecting mental, behavioral, and physical issues, potentially causing diseases like diabetes, suicide, depression, or diabetes is astounding. What is most pressing is no governmental plans, actions, or realistic steps to reunite displaced migrant children with parents. Hiding these children all over the country, in effect terminating parental rights to children of all ages, goes beyond violating the Constitution and human rights.

In memory of the Holocaust, countless lives were lost as other countries did not get involved. The Nazi regime tried to portray a reality that the concentration camps were summer camps like one network tried to allude to. The longer the separation continues of the children and migrant adults, the potential for more harmful effects on these families.

Can we afford to sit back and wait for a midterm election to take action against an unjust administration? What is Congress going to do to prevent a callous administration from acting out of whim, without intellect, without reflection, and on the direction of a seriously flawed and immature leader? As our allies in Britain, Canada, and other countries are dismayed at the creation of migrant internment camps separating adults from children and treating migrants as criminals, how can our own country's leaders not take action to impeach this POTUS, not only for this human rights crisis created by this administration, but previous transgressions?

Simone Ilese

6/22/2018

Dear Congress,

While Special Prosecutor Mueller has to complete the investigation on the Russia probe, the crime of obstruction of justice is blatantly obvious. Why does the POTUS constantly protect the Russian president, enable Russia, not investigate the Russian interference into the U.S. election, and state on public media that he fired Comey because of the Russia probe? At the same time, the administration contradicts itself by stating it fired Comey because of the past handling of the investigation of the Hillary Clinton emails that helped him get elected. It does not take a rocket scientist to see the inconsistency and lack of credibility.

We should no longer be surprised at the lies, inconsistencies, and exaggerations by the POTUS to justify wrongs, blaming Democrats and other countries for not taking responsibility. The total disregard for environmental safety by backing out of the Paris Accord with allies is a disgrace, and demonstrates the pattern of respecting dictators over allies. Blaming Democrats for lack of protection of DACA recipients and mistreatment of migrant families seeking asylum, coming through Mexico, is a pattern of diverting responsibility from the administration that created the crisis. Blaming the FBI and democratic institutions for overstepping boundaries for completing the Russia investigation into potential crimes by the POTUS, his family, and administration is a diversion that only a guilty defendant would use.

If the Mueller investigation is sitting on evidence that is worse than we think it is because, after all, we do not have all of the evidence in yet, why are we not seriously contemplating impeachment proceedings yet?

Simone Ilese

6/22/2018

Dear Congress,

It no longer feels like the United States of America, but more like the Divided States of America. Even as we are divided, we can agree on some principles. While many value the sanctity of human lives, why cannot we put ourselves in the shoes of other people?

The recent shooting of an unarmed teenager in Pittsburgh is horrifying! The young man was shot three times fleeing, not attacking anyone. How many more shootings of unarmed black teenagers can continue before real changes in gun control policy and policing policies and procedures with more diversity training before changes take place?

While the current administration creates and disingenuous appearance that it support human lives through abolishing abortion and capital punishment, what about the sanctity of preserving all human lives of all races, origins, and backgrounds?

How can we work to rectify racism, antisemitism, and discrimination against women and minorities in this country when so many problems are facing an administration in such disarray? Also, when the current administration enables and promotes attitudes of bigotry, hatred, and stereotypes, how can we go forward as a nation, instead of backwards on so many important issues of social justice? Racist attitudes are just as dangerous as racist actions. As an example, take a look at the current POTUS's past false attacks on President Obama not being a U.S. citizen perpetrating years of hatred, bigotry, and discrimination without any factual basis.

With the focus on a corrupt administration with so many moral and legal actions and scrutiny, there have been little or no improvements in policing since the Trayvon Martin tragedy of our times.

Simone Ilese

6/24/2018

My Word: What happens in jury room stays there

July 31, 2013|By Simone Ilese

While the legal side of me is not shocked at the George Zimmerman not-guilty verdict, the emotional side of me is outraged. I was hoping for a manslaughter conviction.

From my past prosecutorial experience in the trenches of many criminal jury trials, I know the reality. One individual in a group with a unique life experience can change the dynamics of a deliberating jury. As attorneys, we rarely learn the mindset of the jurors and the reason for the decision. What goes on in the jury room to finalize the verdict is usually a mystery, as it is the sacred right of the jurors to remain silent.

The Zimmerman jury started out as three not-guilty votes and three guilty votes, with two for manslaughter. As this exemplifies, predicting a jury verdict is like rolling the dice. Luck plays a role in it. Why did three who decided guilty verdicts change their minds? Did a more controlling and outspoken juror overpower the others with her will?

Could any juror have felt so pressured or exhausted after hours of deliberation that she compromised her will? Should the final verdict have been a hung jury? Would there be a different verdict if the talented prosecutors had hammered in the law and elements of crime more meticulously in closing arguments?
Through hearing witness Rachel Jeantel, the voice of the victim revealed he was worried after being followed by Zimmerman and was trying to get away, saying, "Get off, get off." What makes the defendant's self-serving story, exaggerated by his criminal-justice studies and knowledge, more credible than Jeantel's testimony?

As Trayvon Martin's father poignantly expressed, if his son had been the defendant in this scenario, he would have been convicted of manslaughter.

If Jeantel, white or black, were more articulate and calmer, would the verdict have been different? Isn't the content of the message more important than how eloquently it was delivered in weighing the credibility of testimony of witnesses?

Did the preconceived ideas, experiences, background of one or two outspoken or strong-minded jurors overtake the weaker ones in the group?

We may never know what went on in the jury room. In the interest of justice, however, it is good that we are talking about this as a nation and examining the inequities in our criminal-justice system.

(Published in Florida newspaper, Letter to Editor July 31, 2013 on Trayvon Martin case)

Dear Congress,

Is the United States in a constitutional crisis? Have we reached that out of control point in our history where the other branches of government are handicapped from protecting our American democracy from an evil, not just ignorant, but dictator like presidency. Some of us are outraged by an immoral POTUS that has no ounce of human decency, who is highly toxic to our democracy.

The POTUS continually disregards national security interests, the highly trained intelligence community and his own advisors. Like a spoiled child, he continually gets away with bad behavior creating an extremely toxic and unsafe environment, not only for America, but the entire world. Submissive to the Russian president and other dictators, he consistently demonstrates anti-American ideals, contrary to our beliefs, history, and national security. Proven to be a pathological liar, why would anyone believe his constant chants of no collaboration with Russia in the election interference. Especially when the current administration has done nothing to investigate Russian interference in our election, and only tried to create an untrue narrative, it will do and say anything to mislead the American public to its advantage.

Does it matter whether the reasons for this are to pacify his base for future votes, protect his personal and future economic interests (future hotels), continue to pursue countless personal conflicting interests involving his family and himself (personally profiting millions of dollars from office of POTUS)? The GOP majority of Congress are tiptoeing around countless egregious transgressions, fearful of acting, or standing up to a tyrant.

A great leader does not defend the Constitution by attacking the ideals that make America great, certainly far from the current administration. By pretending to uphold the Constitution by falsely claiming to be the protector against taking the rights of gun owners away, taking credit for protecting Americans against false narratives, the POTUS continues to divide Americans. Until Congress steps up against the current administration with unity, we will not live up to the name of the United States of America.

Simone Ilese

6/28/2018

Dear Congress,

If a President cannot act properly and handle the job, isn't it time for Congress to take action? To just sit back and let it happen is unacceptable. Take a look at past history, where immoral acts continued like segregation, the Holocaust…and it took a long time before anyone intervened.

It is pathetic to hear news media broadcasters appeal to the POTUS's family to do the right thing. It is unfair to rely on private institutions to rescue these children separated from their immigrant parents seeking asylum.   The majority of migrant families are not criminals, drug dealers, and rapists, but are good human beings seeking safety.

Even if the children are returned to their parents, the reality of short and long term effects on the brain affecting mental, behavioral, and physical issues are astounding. Is the government, specifically the current administration, contributing to the future physical diseases like diabetes, suicide, substance abuse problems, etc. of the separated children? What is most pressing is no governmental action or little action to take realistic steps to reunify displaced children with parents.

Even with a judicial order for the government to take steps to reunify the children with parents and an extension, there is no assurance every one of the over 2,000 separated children will be successfully reunited. Terminating parental rights of migrant children goes beyond violating the Constitution, the dignity of human rights, and the history of American values.

Simone Ilese

July 2018

Dear Congress,

The current administration and POTUS uses lies, inconsistencies, and exaggerations to justify its wrongs, blaming Democrats and other countries, but never taking responsibility.

The Presidential administration is not a realistic presidency, but a reality T.V. show. Concerned with photo-ops and media appearances, blue wave midterm primaries, to paint its show, it has no interest in correcting its countless misrepresentations, wrongs, and transgressions. The jacket displaying the message, "I really don't care, do you?" says it all.

The administration does not really care about humanity, the migrant children, or Americans. It is only about appearances and caring about their own political safety and personal interests. There is no genuine showing of compassion towards the separated children or anyone except the base that will continue to support them.

Simone Ilese

July 2018

Dear Congress,

What a shame that GOP leaders conducted a sham hearing to attack the FBI in an effort to shut down Mueller's Russia investigation. It was blatantly obvious what the chairman of the hearing was trying to use an FBI agent to discredit the probe into collusion between Russian and the POTUS. While there was no factual basis to support this hearing, it was clearly an effort to try derail any investigation into the POTUS and deceive the American people.

While the GOP leaders who ran the hearing went out of their way to make the FBI agent Strzok look biased and not credible, they failed miserably. In light of recent indictments of many Russian operatives, the GOP hearing members made of mockery of themselves.

The outcome of this hearing was that the FBI remained strong, unbiased, and credible. The POTUS and his administration remained corrupt in their ways of disgracing our country every day, disrespecting our allies (ex: increased tariff's with Canada), violating the emolument clause, offering little aid to Puerto Rico, disregarding gun control and creating distractions, not betterment for Americans.

Simone Ilese

7/12/2018

Dear Congress,

It is a sad day in American history when you have a POTUS on foreign soil standing next to a dictator, acting as his puppet, and defending that dictator's attacks against the U.S. while attacking America's institutions and intelligence agencies. The American intelligence that Russian interfered with our election is based on details and facts. The POTUS's refusal to stand up to the Russian president's denial of interference in our recent election is a disgrace.

By meeting with the Russian leader without any record keepers for a lengthy time, the POTUS, in fact, was openly colluding with the Russian president, in contrast to his constant offers of no collusion. While the POTUS has a pattern of doing the opposite of what he says he does, his words can never be trusted as true or based on facts. The POTUS has less credibility than his dictator counterpart who is honest about wanting the current POTUS elected. Like the Russian president, he most likely lies about ever having previous contact with his counterpart.

Does the POTUS refuse to admit that Russia and its president interfered with our recent election and attack our institutions because he is insecure with the legitimacy of his presidency since he did not win the popular vote against Hillary Clinton? Does he ingratiate, pacify, and elevate the Russian president because he puts his own interests of pursuing development in Russia or illegal activities before America's interests and national security? Is he submissive to Russia because its president has information that could damage him with his base? Does he continually elevate the Russian president over NATO leaders because he secretly admires dictator like leadership and wishes that for himself? Is the POTUS as naïve and grossly incompetent in the office as it is so glaringly obvious? Perhaps, it is all of the above. No matter what it is that motivates the POTUS to act this way, he is noticeably combative with everyone (U.S. intelligence agencies, past and current democrats or opposition from the GOP, administration advisors, Hillary Clinton).

The only operatives he is not combative are the dictators that attack our democracy. Similarly, the POTUS elevated the white supremacists in Charlottesville at the same level of culpability as the victims. Shouldn't there be more than criticism from some members of Congress, but rather a movement of uproar and call for action?

By elevating a dictator that recently attacked our democracy and attacking our American institutions on the world stage in Finland, doesn't this demonstrate an act of treason committed by the POTUS at the summit with Russia? If this does not rise to the level of high crimes and misdemeanor or unfitness for presidential office, it is seriously questionable what would it take? Is Congress listening? When is Congress going to act?

Simone Ilese

7/16/2018

Dear Congress,

The world is watching the Brett Kavanaugh confirmation hearing including the testimony of Dr. Christine Blasey Ford. Please vote "No" against the confirmation of Brett Kavanaugh to the Supreme Court. To vote otherwise would be supporting that Dr. Blasey Ford's testimony is not believable. That would be an outrageous conclusion.

Dr. Blasey Ford, a clinical psychologist was most credible in her testimony recounting a sexual assault by Brett Kavanaugh. She unequivocally identifies and remembers that Kavanaugh attempted to rape her when she was 15 and he was age 17. Not only was she able to explain it in professional terms, but she was compelling in layman's terms. There was no feigning of her emotions at the hearing on 9/27 before the Senate Judiciary committee and the world.

On the other hand, nominee Kavanaugh's testimony was contrived, feigned, not truthful, and self-serving. Even as a federal judge for 12 years, his testimony was not a display of judicial temperament. It was obvious he was belligerent, condescending, not only in his demeanor and tone, but in his words and responses mostly to the female Democrats on the committee. A quote from Maya Angelou is relevant, "I've learned that people will forget what you said, people will forget what you did, but people will never forget how you made them feel." The long lasting feelings from the sexual assault has not left this victim, Dr. Blasey Ford, for over 35 years. As you compare their testimonies, Dr. Blasey Ford's account is far more credible than the Supreme Court nominee, and by his persona, you can visualize her story. If her account is true, then Kavanaugh is lying.

Even if you cannot vote against the confirmation based on Dr. Ford's testimony alone, how could you vote "yes" to such credible testimony that the Supreme Court nominee Kavanaugh sexually assaulted her when he was age 17, without doing more investigation before voting on issue of confirmation? Kavanaugh's actions through the years were not normal teen or young adult behavior. In addition, there are accounts and witnesses that would support other acts of sexual misconduct by this Supreme Court nominee. If Kavanaugh wants fairness and both sides heard, why does he continually evade questions regarding an FBI investigation? The victim most certainly wants an investigation by the FBI to make her testimony more helpful and to question additional witnesses.

Nobody should be laughing at Dr. Blasey Ford and any victim of sexual assault...it would take a depraved mentality to think otherwise...why do people project on others what they are actually guilty of? In times of normalcy, wouldn't Kavanaugh be pulled from consideration as a nominee for a lifetime appointment as a Supreme Court Justice because he would not pass vetting for the job, but times are anything but normal. If we look at the bigger picture, the current administration and POTUS are desperate to save their reign for power over principle of due process and respect for the job as justice of the Supreme Court.   How is the emphasis by the GOP and POTUS on concern for ruining Kavanaugh's life more important than a Supreme Court candidate nominee with serious sexual assault allegations whose judgment could affect millions of American women and men for decades?

Simone Ilese

9/28/2018

Epilogue of Dear Congress by Simone Ilese:

Initially, I used my writing in e-mailed letters to Congress as a way to vent my anger and frustration at the current state of America due to the current occupant of the presidential office.

Realizing that my e-mailed letters to Congress were probably not read by the legislators themselves, it was important for me to participate in the democratic process. Even though I usually received detailed responses, they were more likely read by congressional staffers as a means to decipher the issues important to constituents. In this era, there were so many issues, it was analogous to patching a bag of water with so many holes.

My emailed letters to Congress were more of a symbolic gesture to raise issues. Perhaps, it makes a difference if more people communicate or send written emailed letters to their congressional leaders.

I chose to not refer to the name of the current POTUS because I did not want to give him more attention than he craves. Whether it is negative or positive attention, he thrives on getting respect that he does not deserve. By now, millions of Americans are tired of hearing his name. Similar to a criminal or terrorist, by not identifying his name, it is a way to depersonalize his status.

As the current administration has no understanding of the rule of law, Constitution, moral and ethical boundaries, it may be a result of a combination of incompetence, ignorance, lack of empathy, and ruthless intentional behavior. Nevertheless, our basic U.S. principles are being attacked. No one is above the law and conflicts of interests that affect our most sacred rights of due process, equality of all people, protection of individuals and national security.

So, I wrote this short book to highlight issues that millions of Americans share in hopes to raise common voices over grave concerns for our country. Also, it is a way of reminding many of us that you are not alone in your opinions. After all, getting involved in my local political groups provided some catharsis in these turbulent political times.   As we worry about our constitutional rights getting slowly stripped away, time is of the essence. I wanted to take a step further to use my First Amendment right through writing my views.